MAGIC EYE®

3D Illusions by Magic Eye Inc.

Andrews and McMeel

A Universal Press Syndicate Company

Kansas City

Printed in the United States of America. Published by Andrews and McMeel, a Universal Press Syndicate Company, 4520 Main Street, Kansas City, Missouri 64111.

ISBN: 0-8362-1332-7

INTRODUCTION

From the moment he was bitten by a radioactive spider, Peter Parker—the amazing Spider-Man—has captured the imagination of generations of fans. Now you can see this Marvel Comics legend for the very first time through the hidden world of Magic Eye! Via the patented Magic Eye process, you can see Spider-Man tackle his most formidable foes. Classic villains like Venom, Hobgoblin, and Carnage, just to name a few, burst out in three dimensions, giving you a powerful feeling of Spider-Man's awesome abilities and evil enemies.

Created by writer/editor Stan Lee and artist Steve Ditko in 1962, Spider-Man quickly caught the notice of people the world over. Enthralled by the adventures of this off-beat, spider-powered, very *human* Super Hero, these people have helped make Spider-Man the stunning success he is today. Currently headlining eight monthly comic book titles (selling over 15 million copies a year in the U.S. alone) and starring in his own Saturday morning animated series on the Fox Kids Network, the wondrous wall-crawler shows no sign of running out of web-fluid!

Likewise, Magic Eye has also taken the world by storm, with twenty book titles and record-breaking sales. The enthusiasm and addiction of Magic Eye fans have proven to be a driving force behind the ongoing success of this 3D phenomenon. From billboards to bubble gum, Magic Eye continues to delight and fascinate the kid in everyone.

Those fabulous 3D artists at Magic Eye Inc., Cheri Smith, Andy Paraskevas, Bill Clark, and Ron Labbe, couldn't have completed this work without collaboration from Ursula Ward, Mike Thomas, and Will Conrad at Marvel. Together they formed a team whose awesome powers can only be rivaled by those of Spider-Man himself!

So sit back in your seat, true believer, and prepare to be pummeled by a pulse-pounding plethora of magnificent, mind-numbing Magic Eye images! 'Nuff said!

NOTE: Pages 31 and 32 of this book provide a key that shows the 3D picture that you'll see when you find and train your Magic Eye.

VIEWING TECHNIQUES

Learning to use your Magic Eye is easier than you might think, and once you get it, it becomes easier and easier. For some people it takes more time than others, so here are a few tips to get you started.

Start off in a quiet place and in a relaxed state. To view these images, it is necessary to hold your gaze long enough to give your brain time to decode the 3D information that has been coded into the repeating patterns by our computer programs. These images are meant to be seen by "diverging" your eyes (separating them); if the image appears sinking instead of floating, you are probably crossing your eyes. If that happens, relax and try again.

Free-viewing 3D images is safe and even potentially helpful to your eyes, but straining will not help and could cause you discomfort. Enjoy yourself, relax, and let the image come to you.

Method One

Hold the image so that it touches your nose. Let the eyes relax and stare vacantly off into space, as if you are looking through the image, not at it; at this point the image will appear blurry. When you are relaxed, move the pages slowly away from your face, perhaps an inch every two or three seconds. Keep looking through the page. Stop at a comfortable reading distance and keep staring. After a few seconds you will perceive depth followed by a 3D image. The most discipline is needed when something starts to "come in," you will instinctively try to look at the page. If you look at it, start again.

Method Two

Place the image behind a clear reflective surface, such as glass or Plexiglas. Look at your reflection, and continue to stare at it with a fixed gaze. The image will appear to develop much like an instant photo.

Method Three

Focus on an object in the distance while holding the image at arms length just below eye level. After staring at the focal point until you become relaxed, slowly raise the image to eye level, while continuing to stare into the distance. The hidden image should then come into focus.

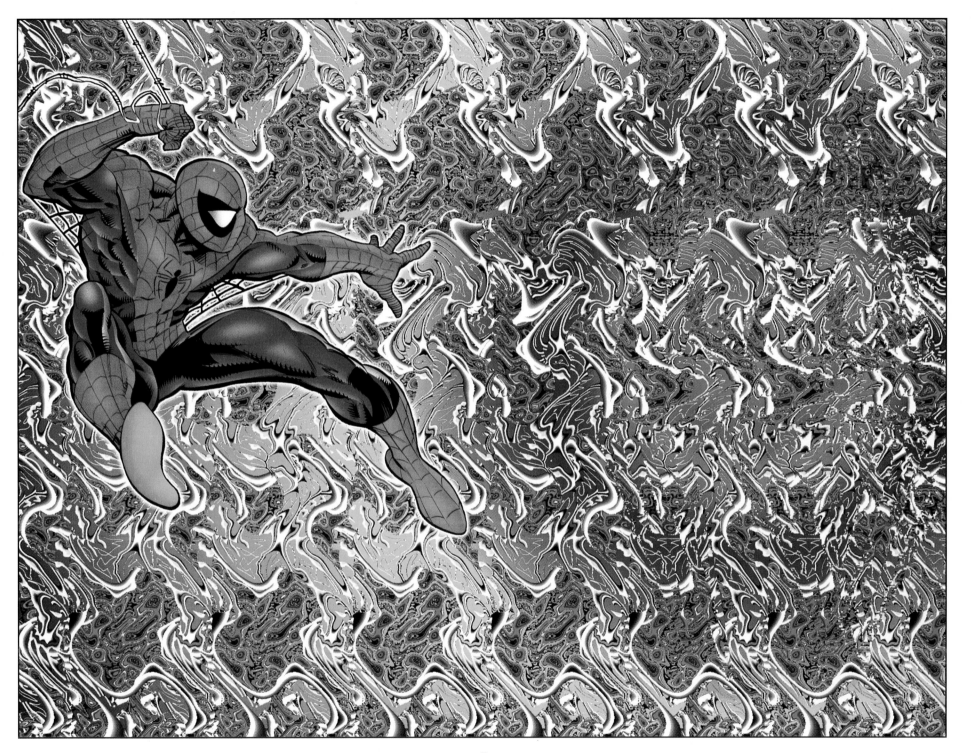

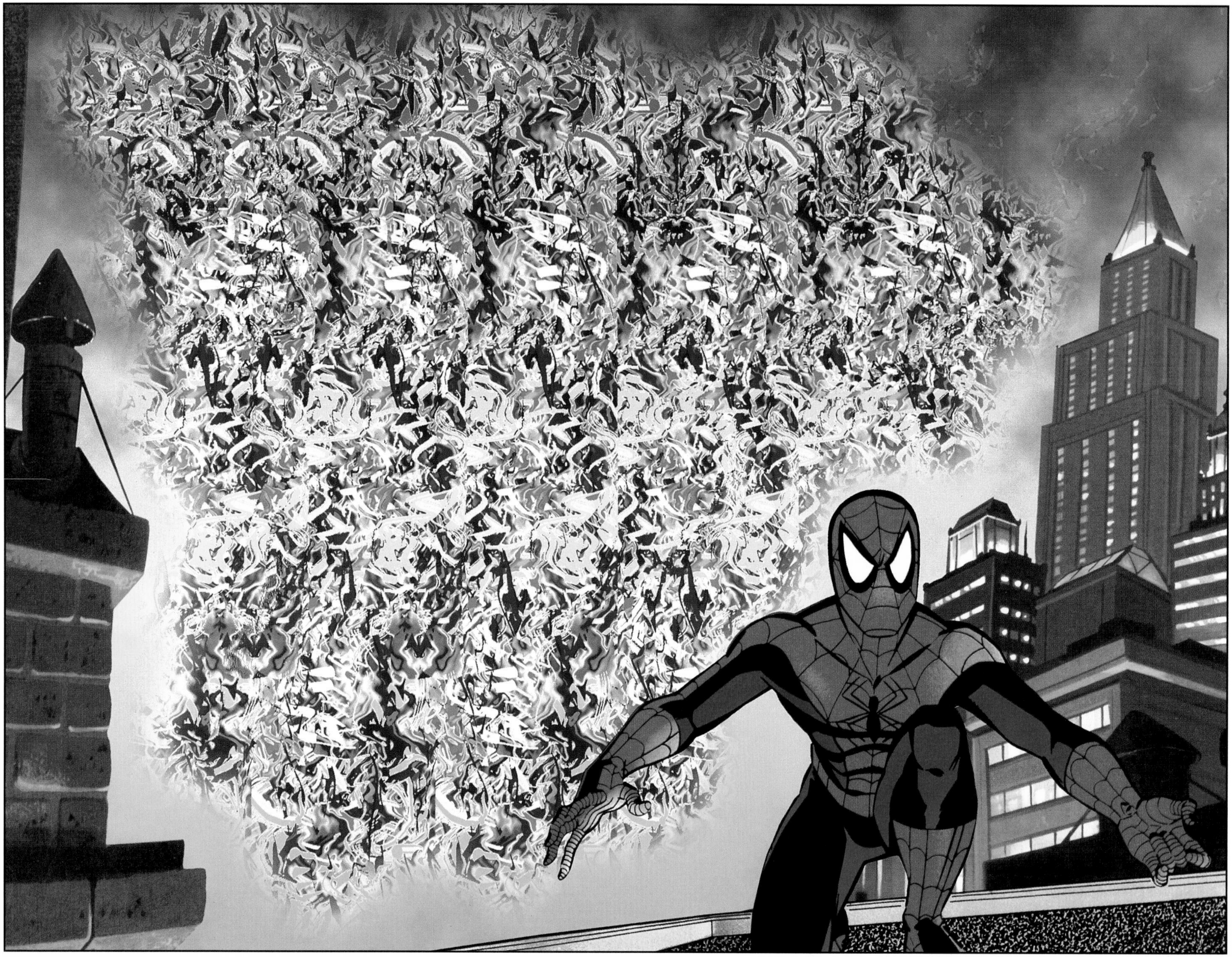

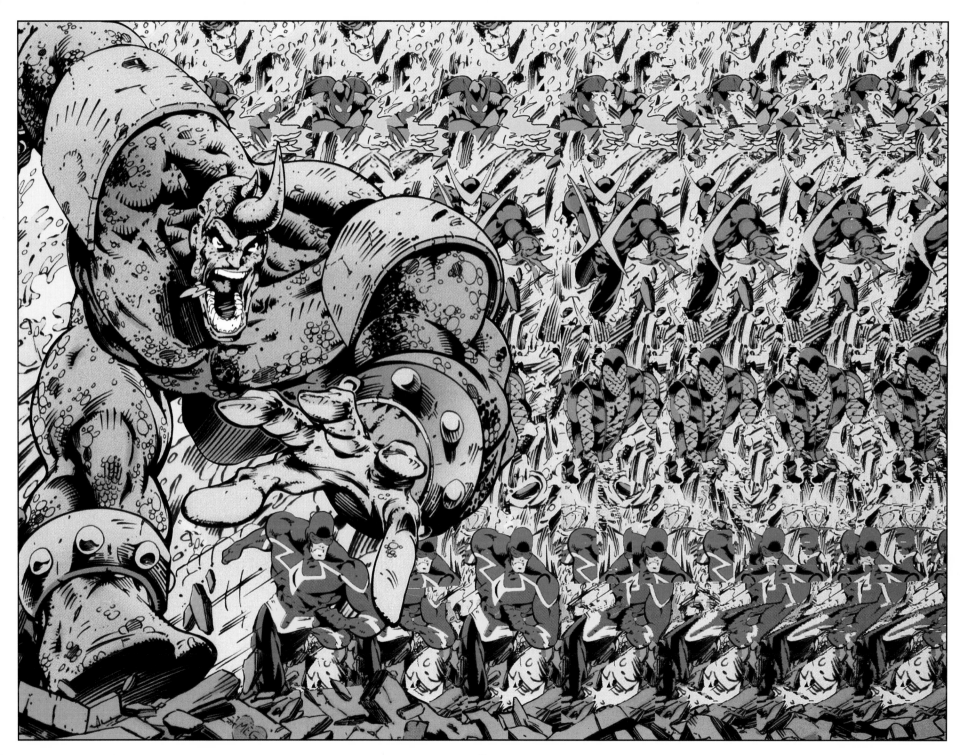

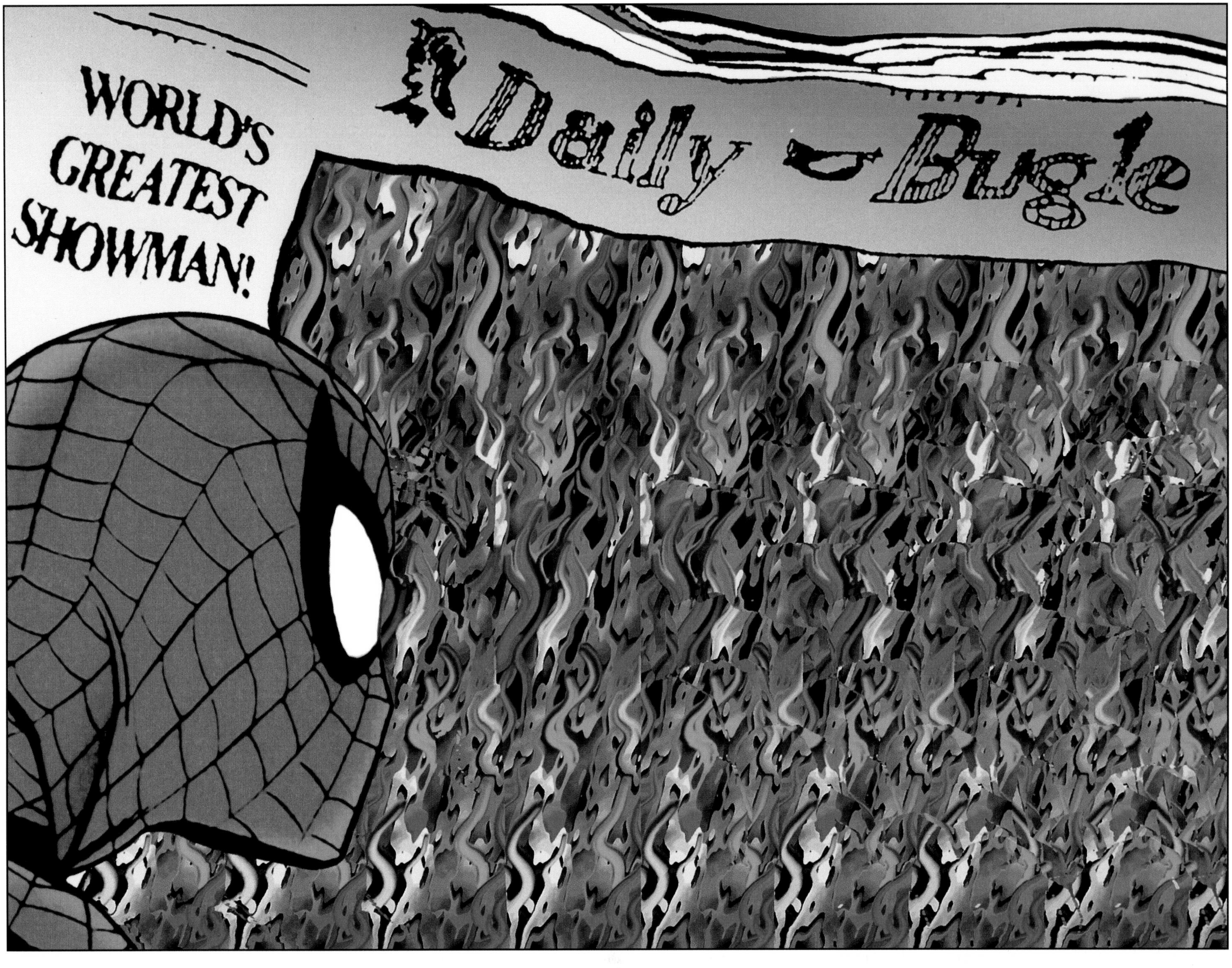
WORLD'S GREATEST SHOWMAN!
Daily Bugle

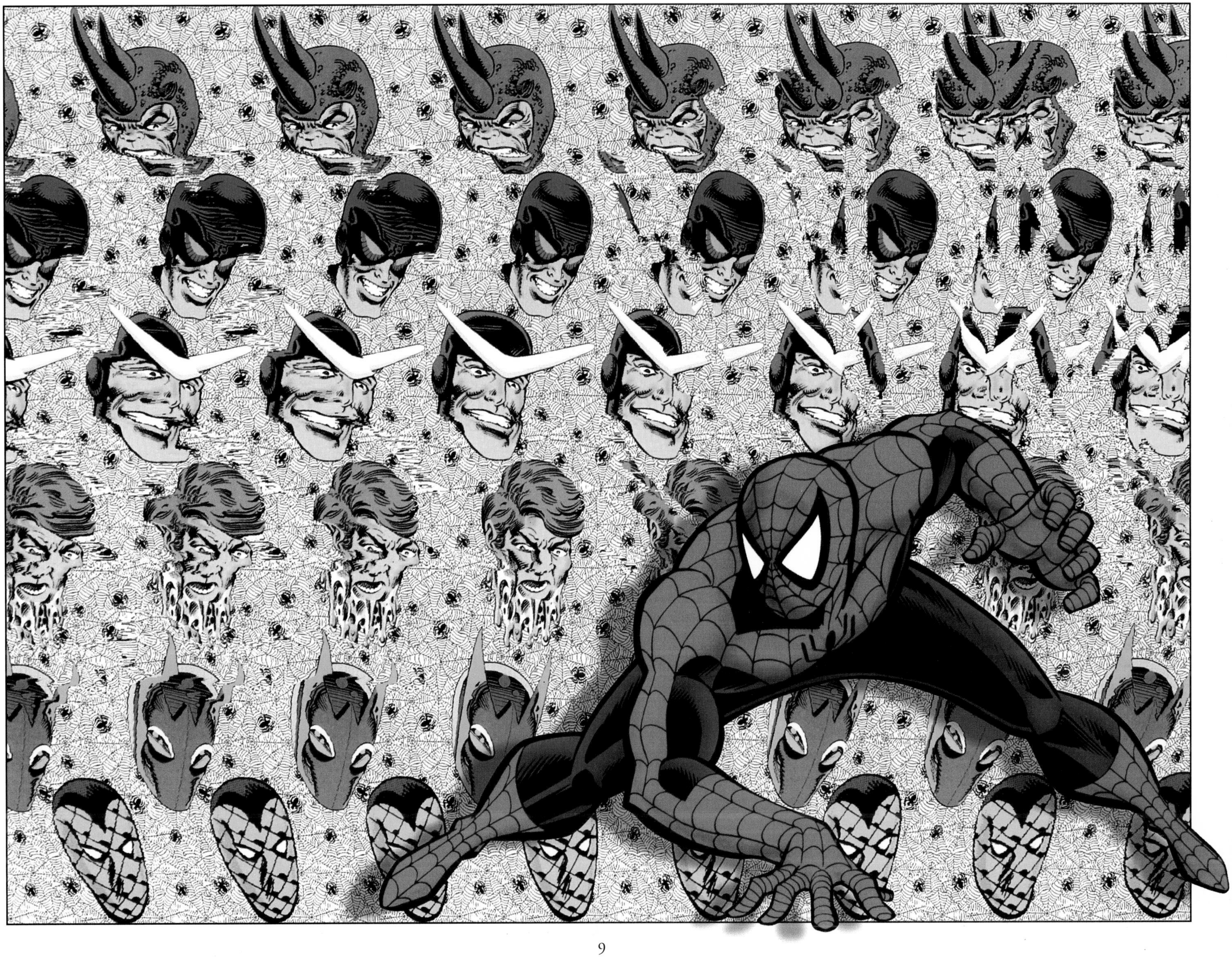

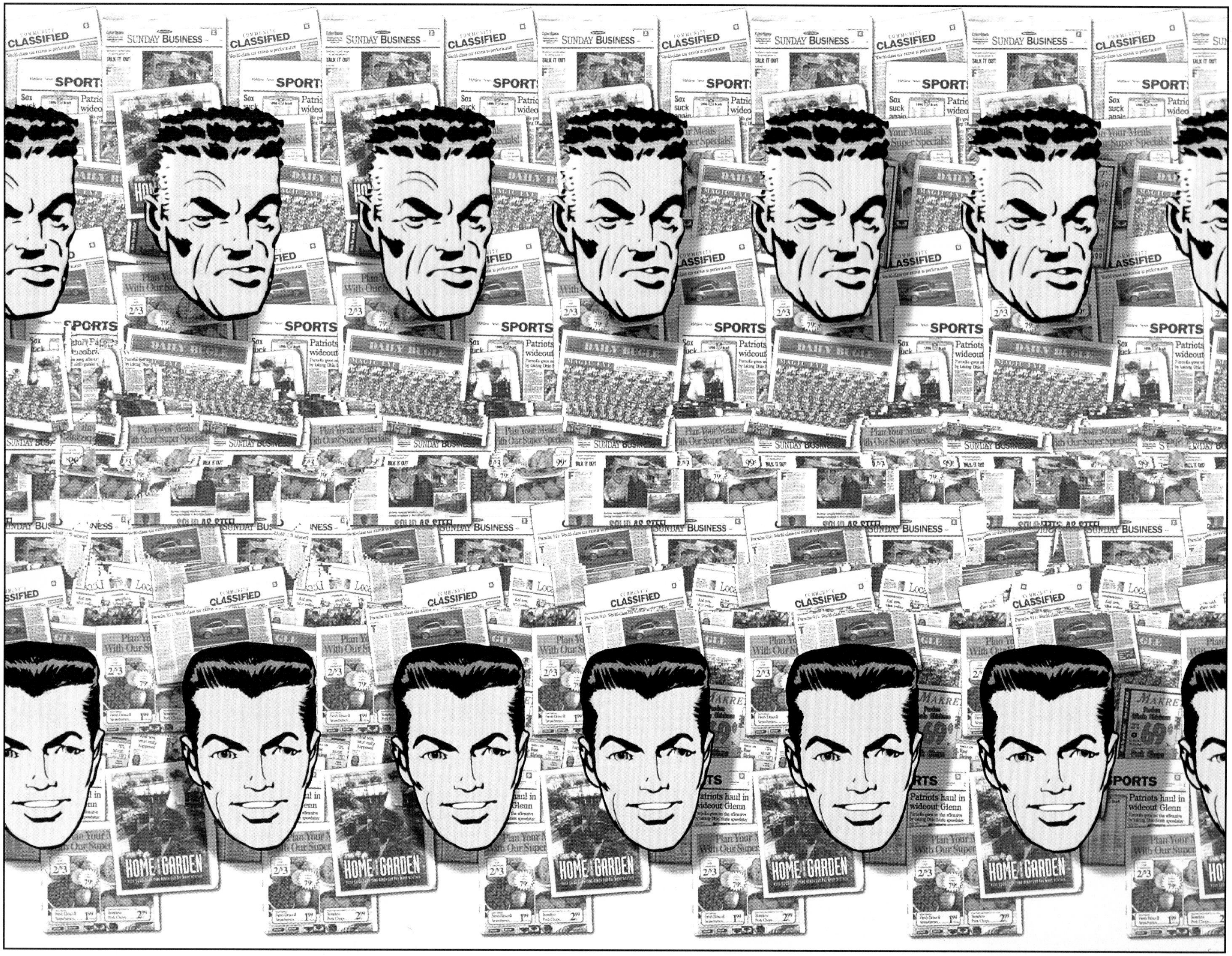
COMMUNITY CLASSIFIED
SUNDAY BUSINESS
SPORTS
DAILY BUGLE
Plan Your Meals With Our Super Specials!
Patriots haul in wideout Glenn
SOLID AS STEEL
HOME GARDEN

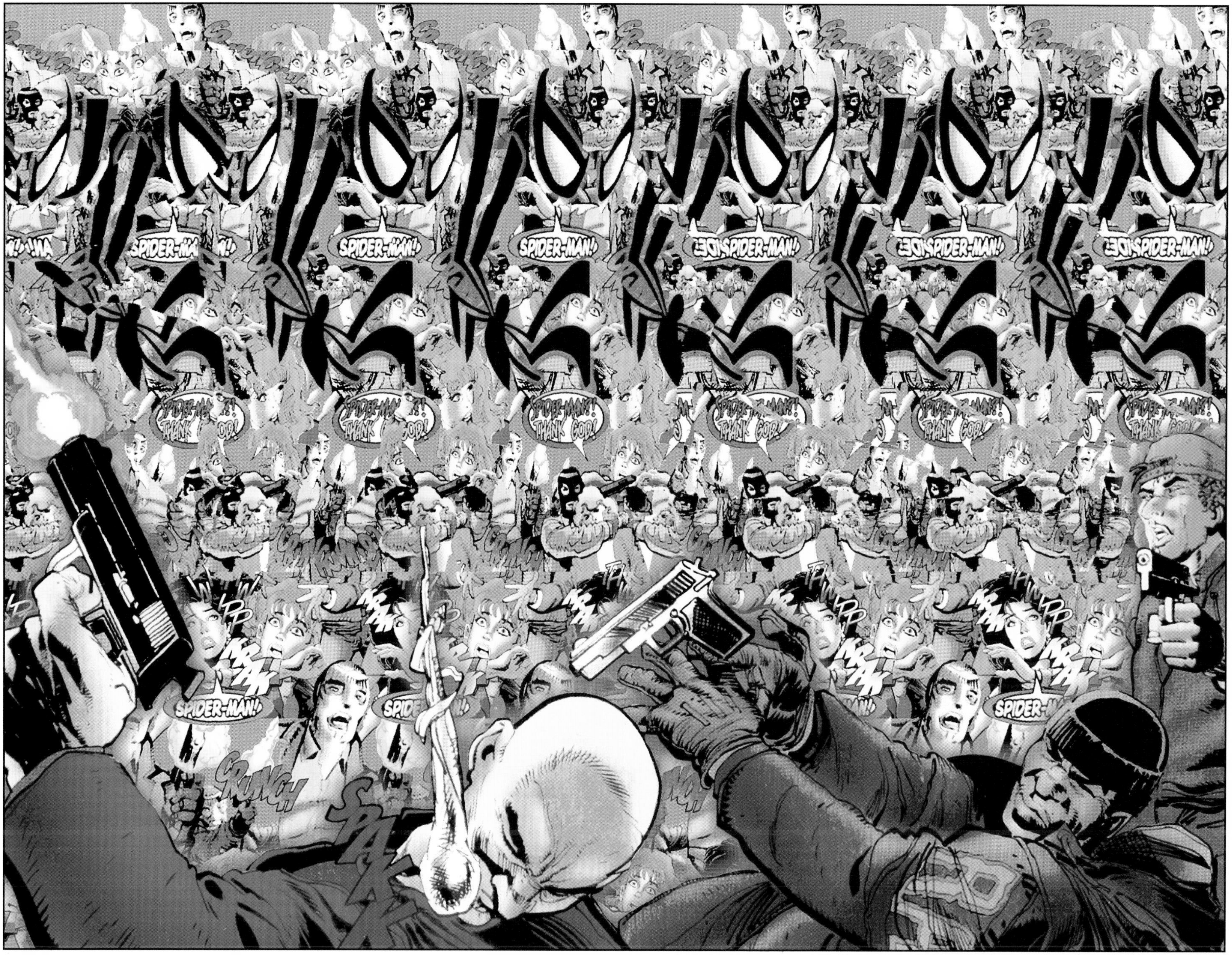
SPIDER-MAN!
CRUNCH

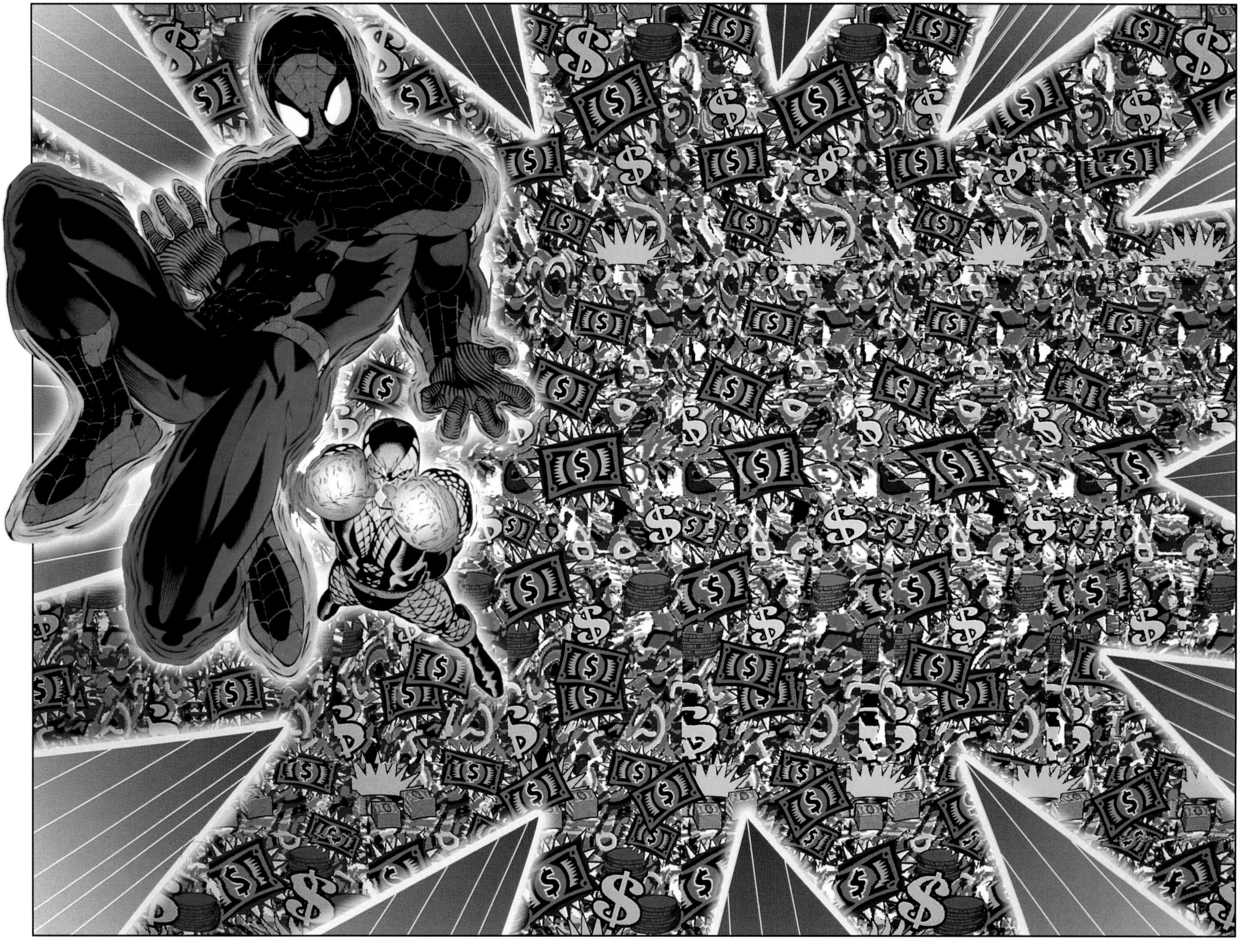

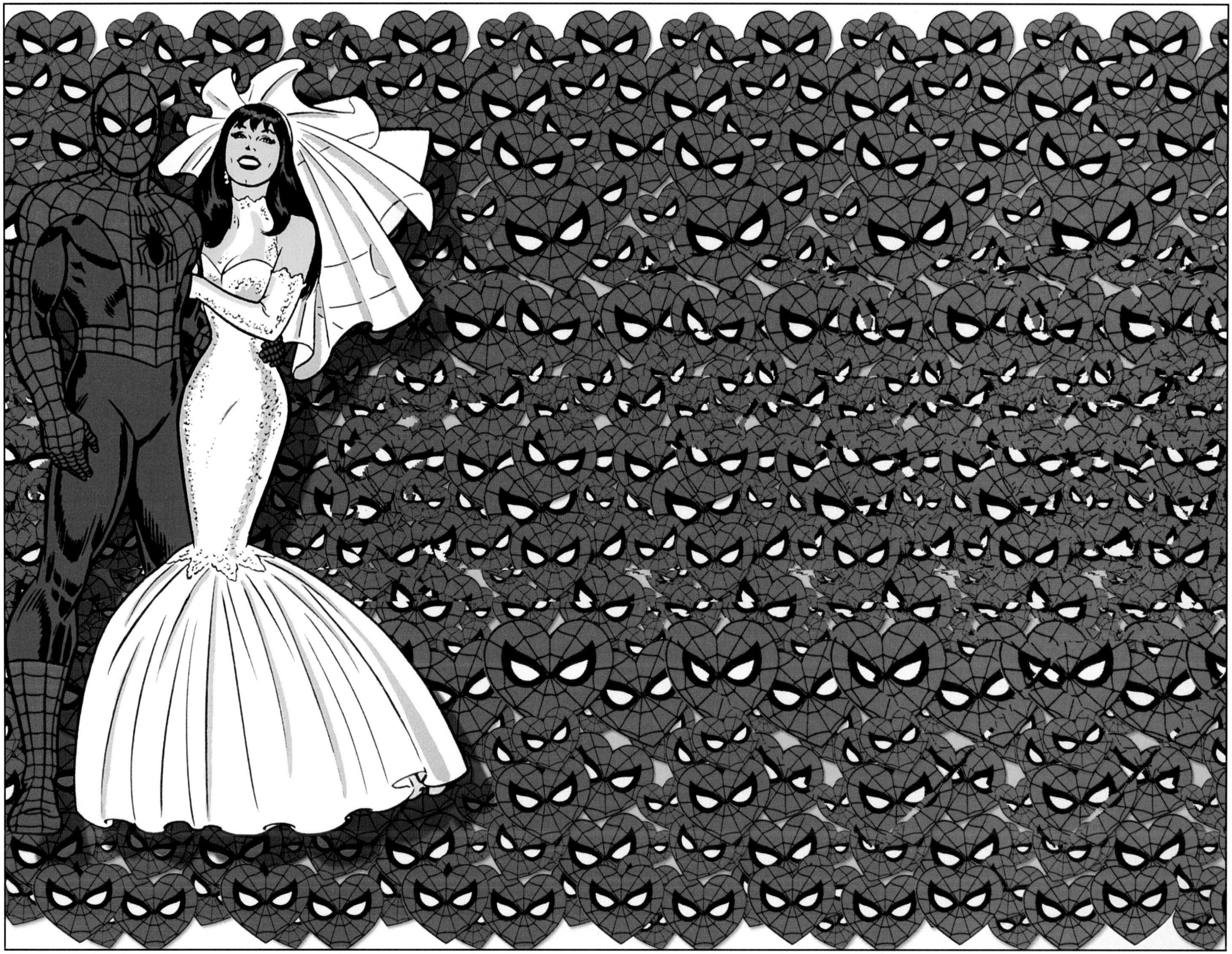

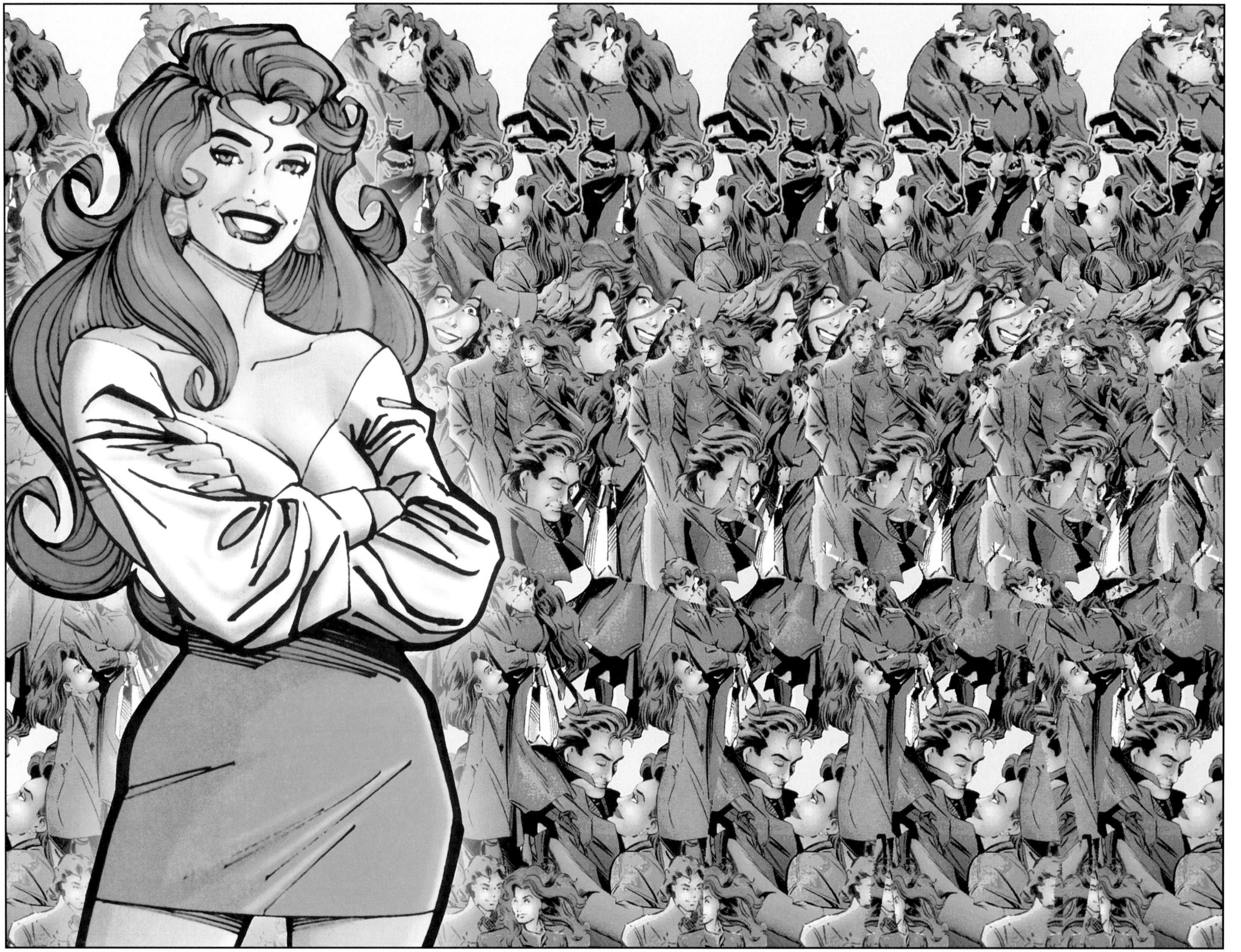

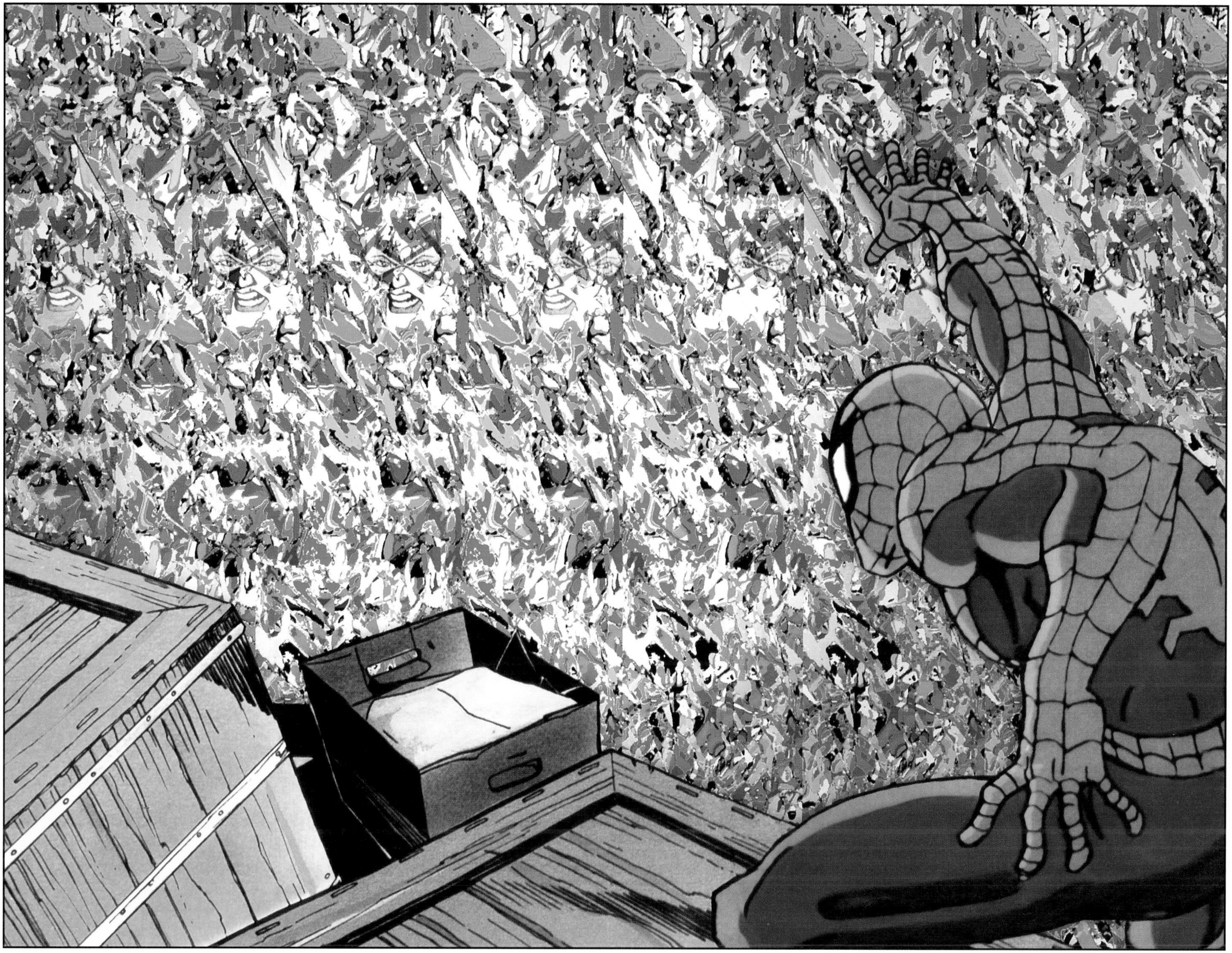

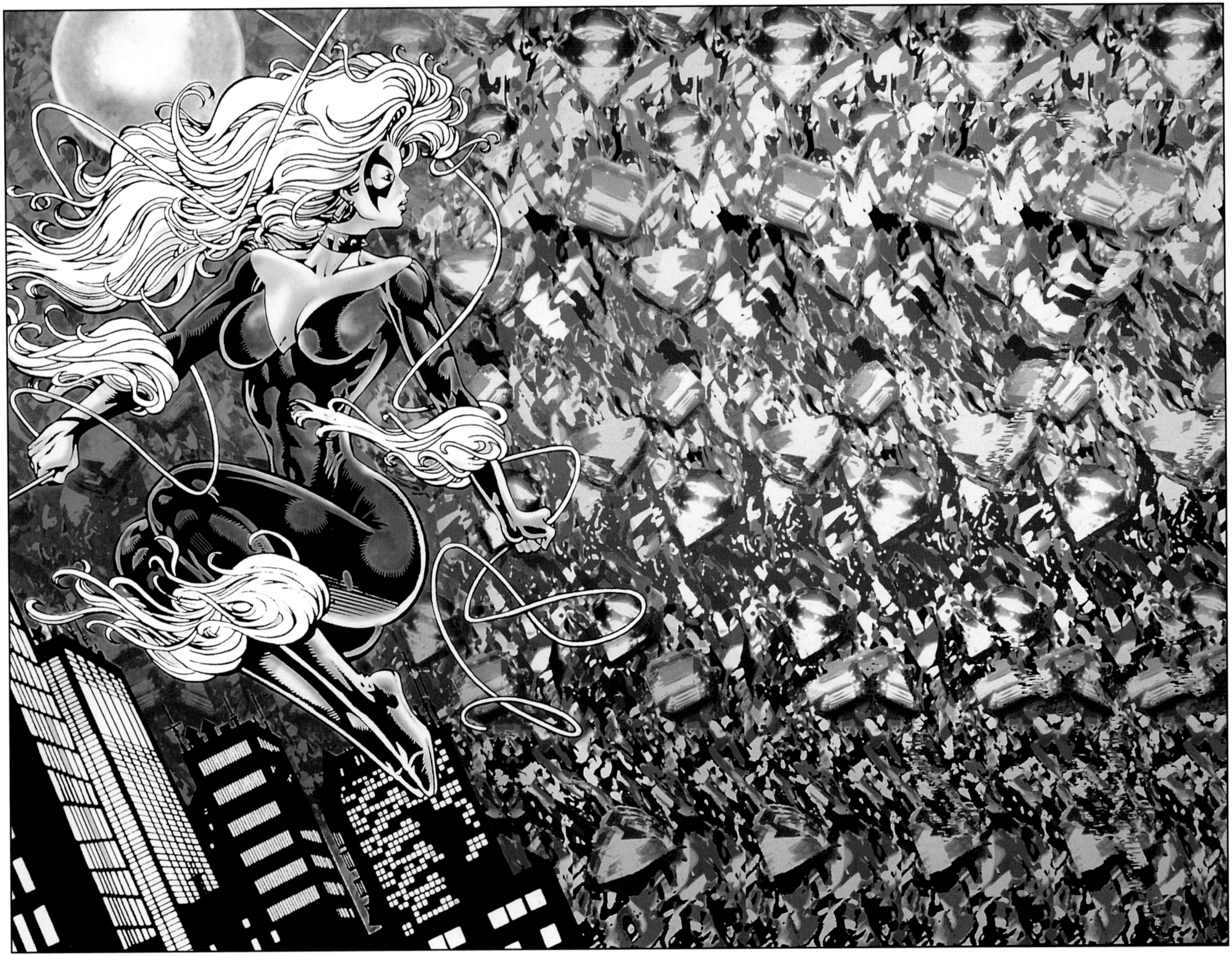

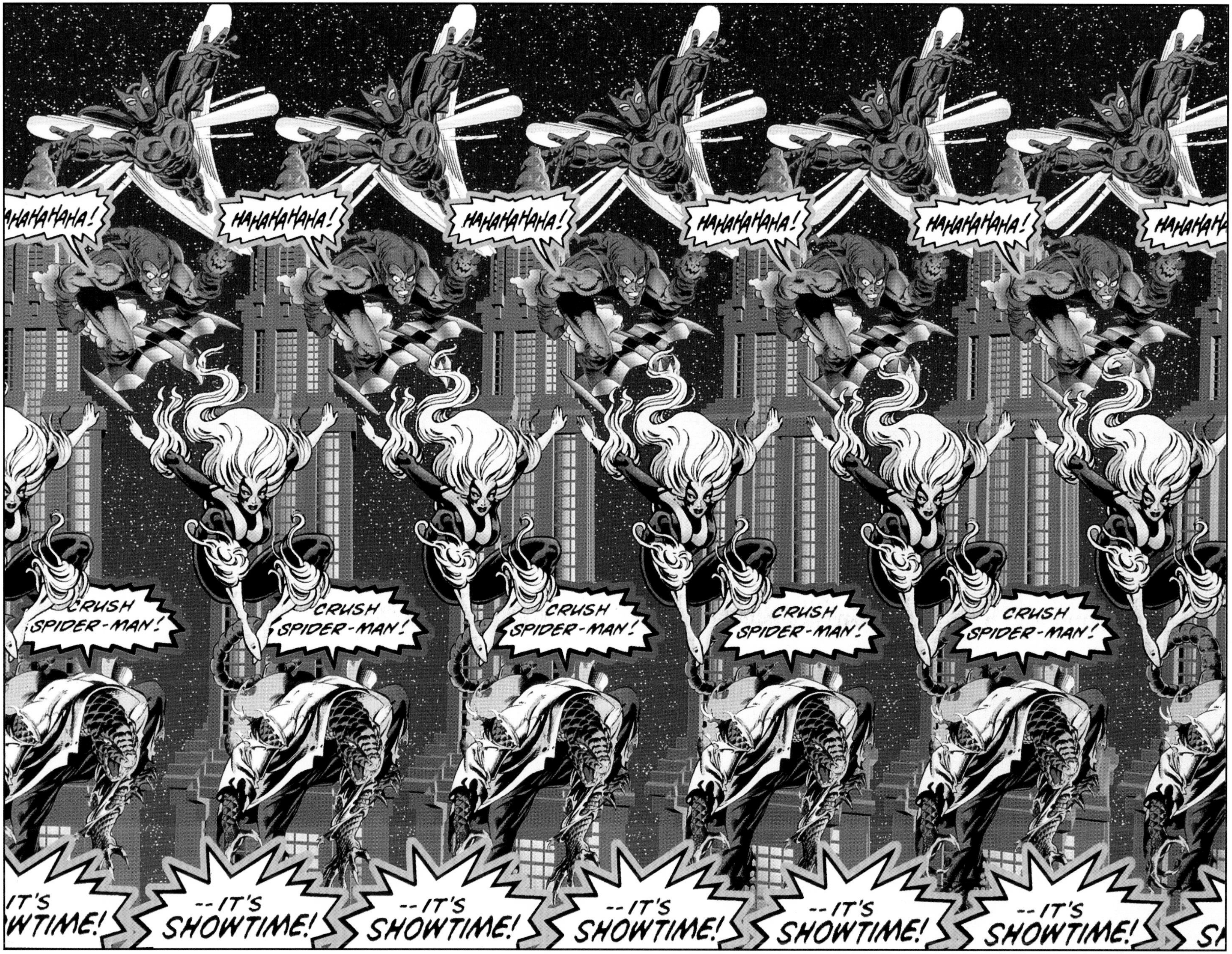
HAHAHAHAHA!
CRUSH SPIDER-MAN!
--IT'S SHOWTIME!

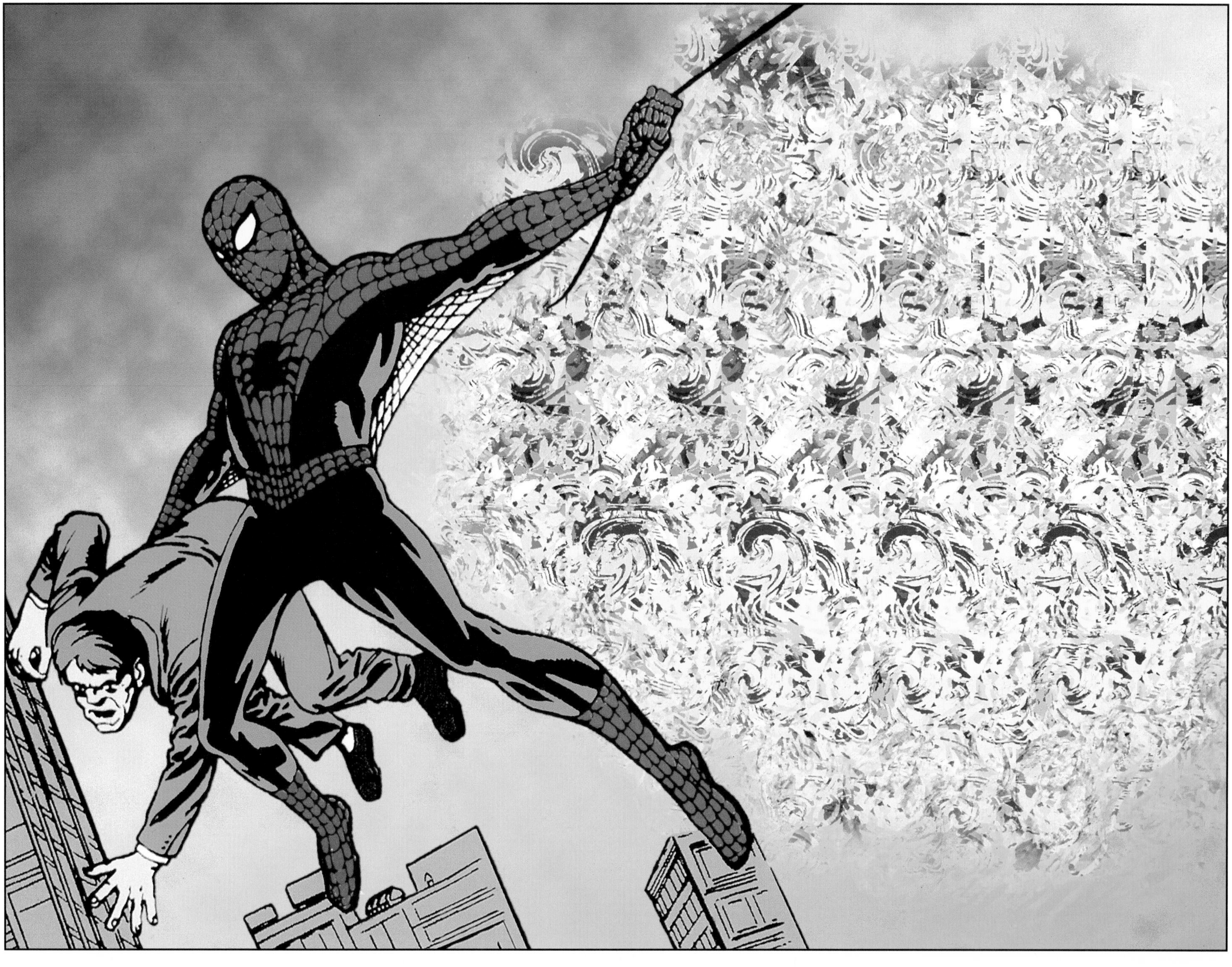

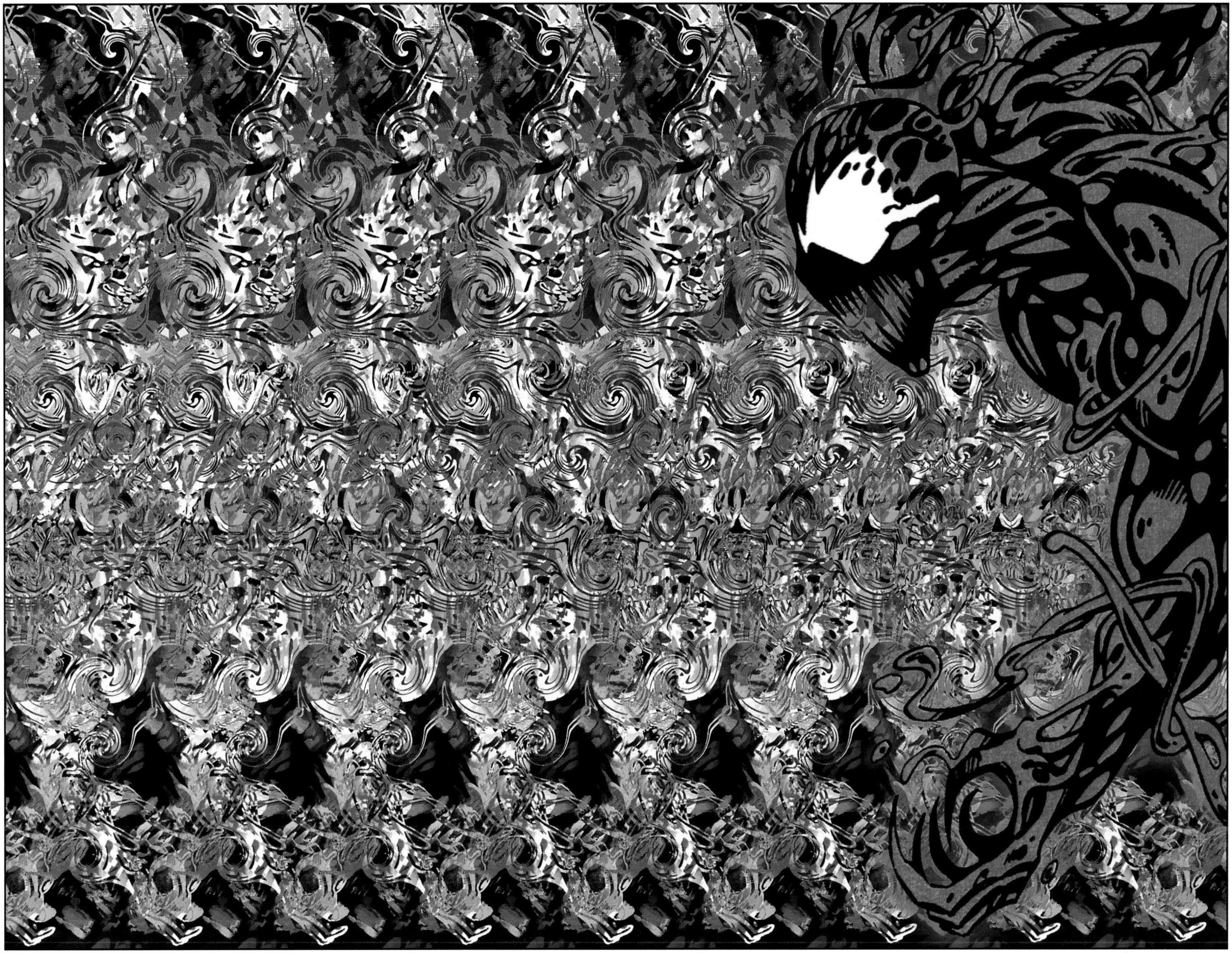

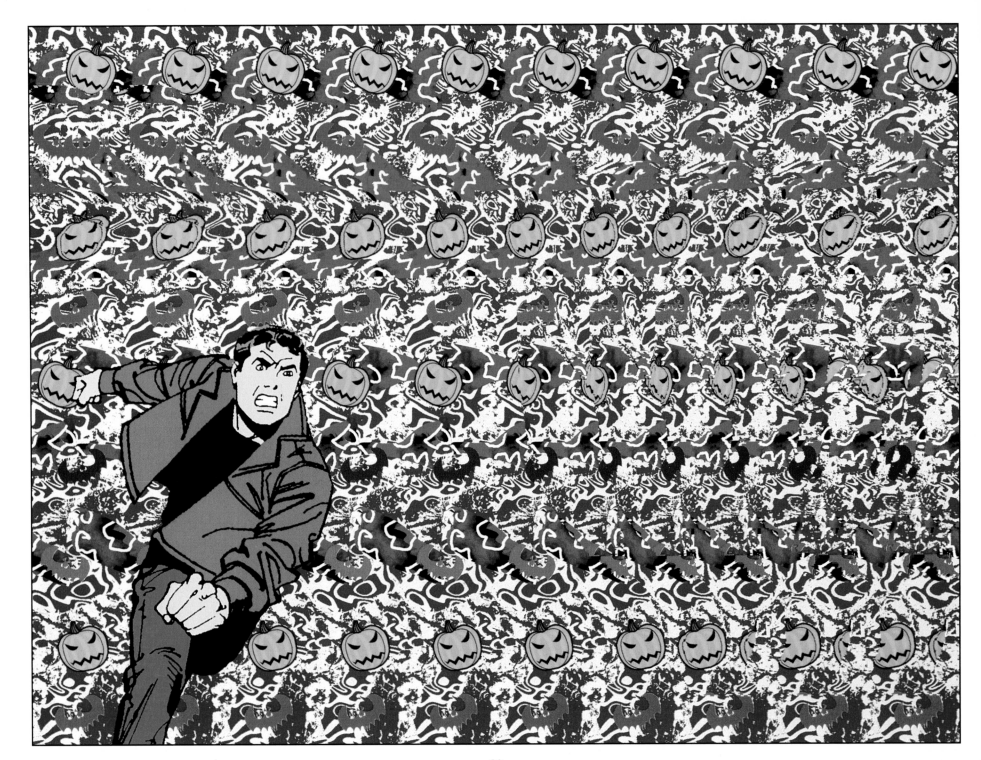

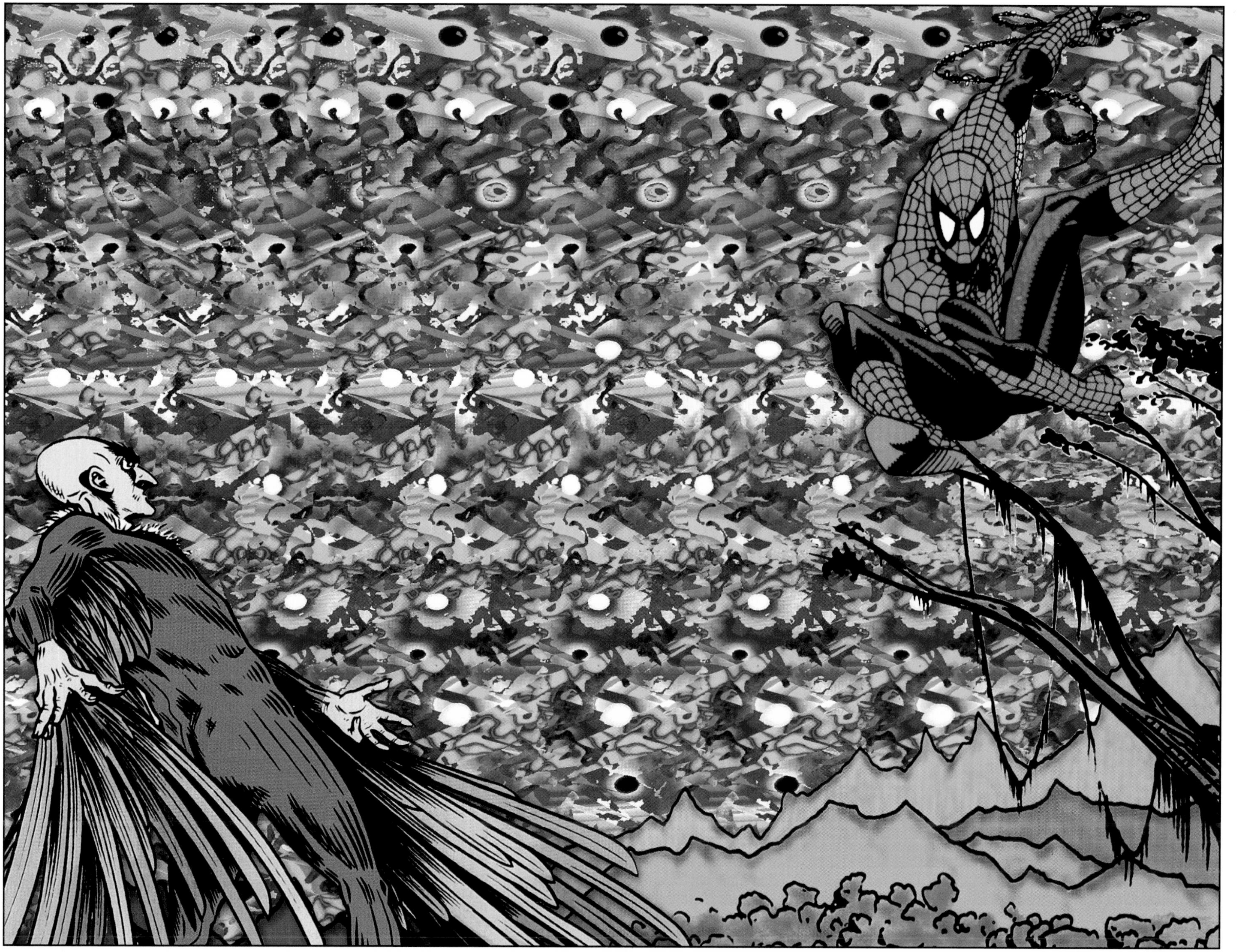

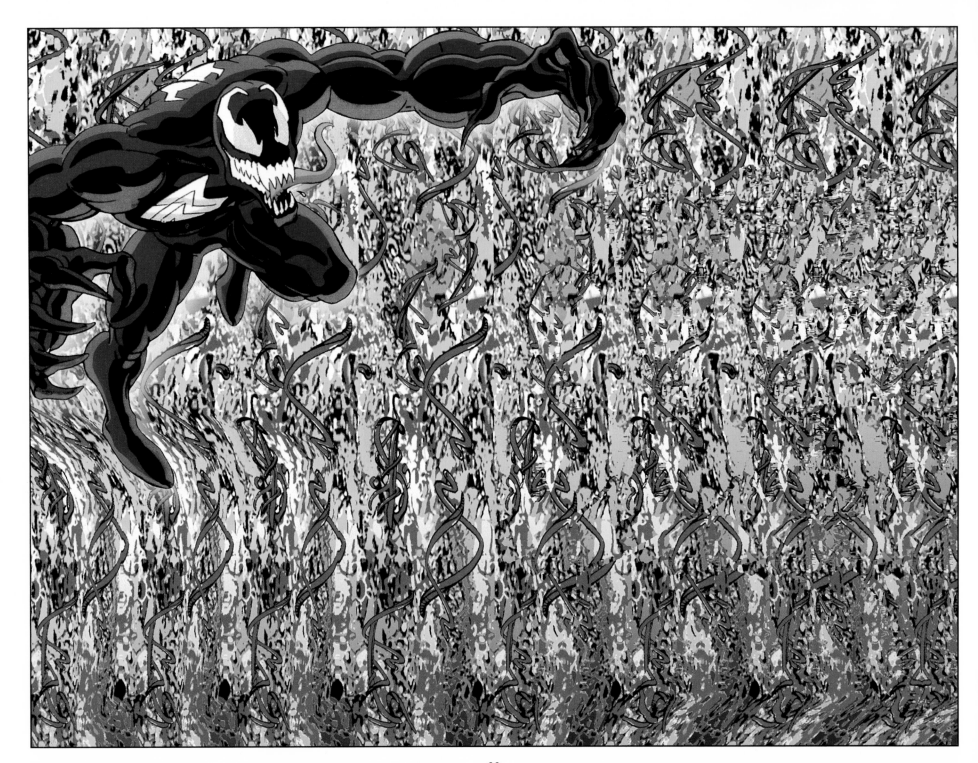

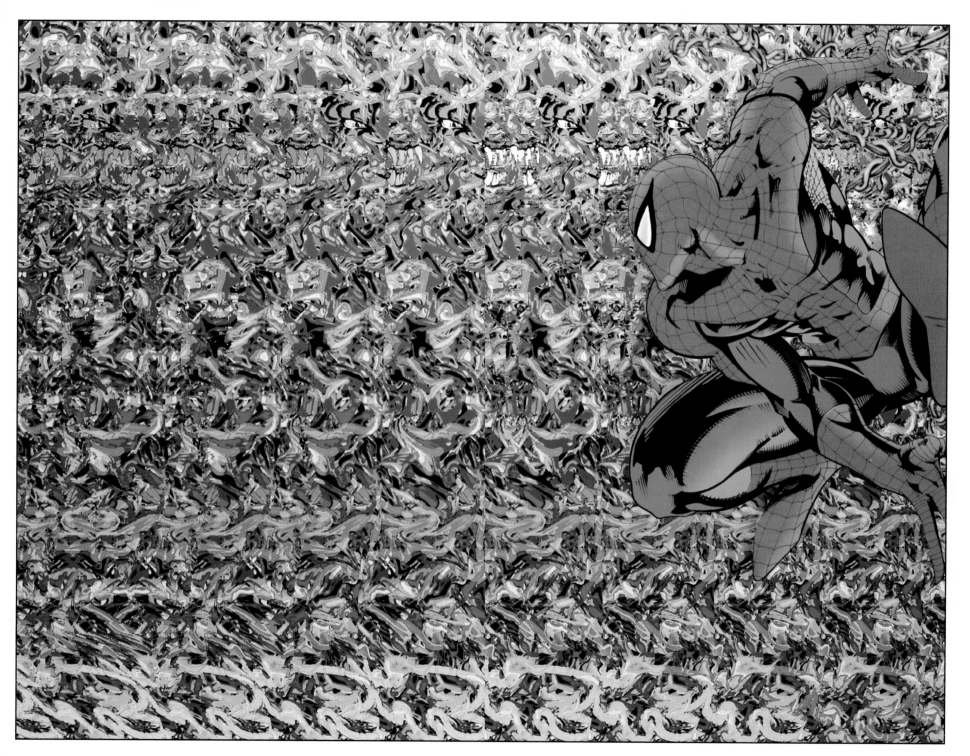

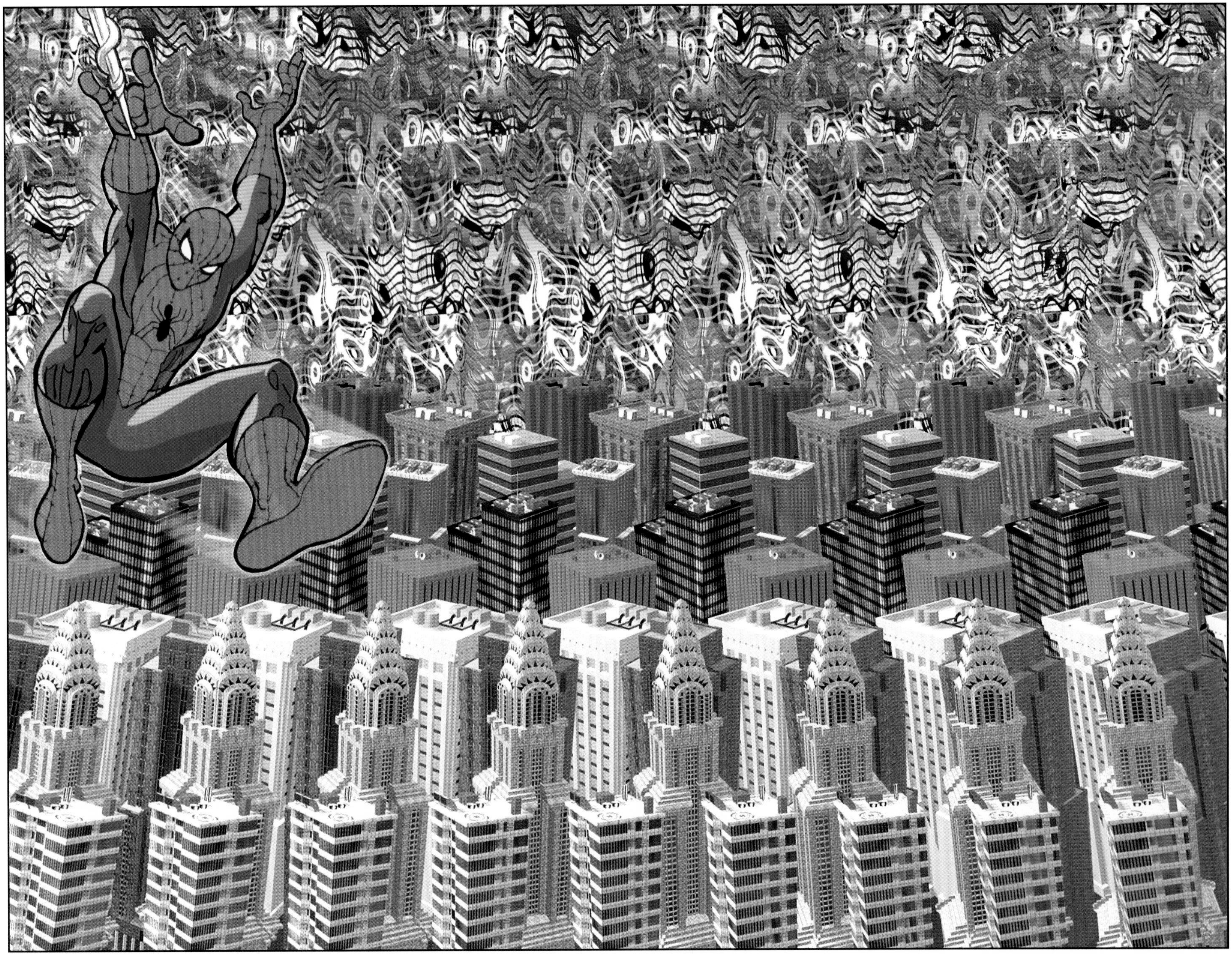

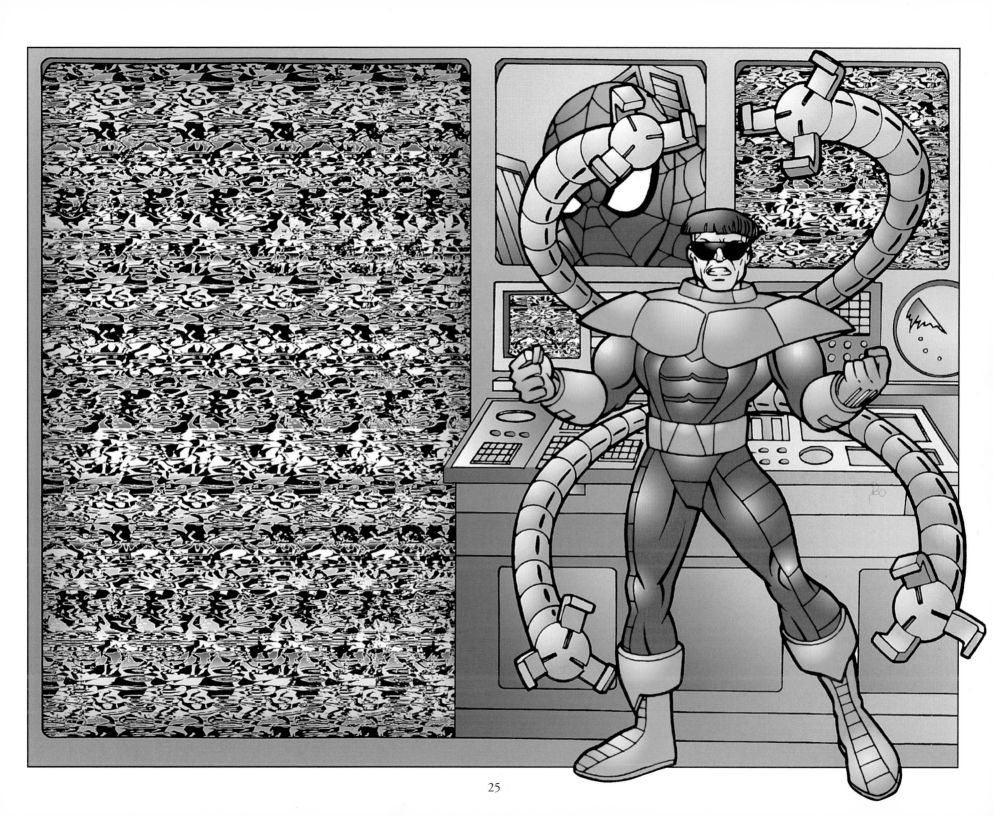

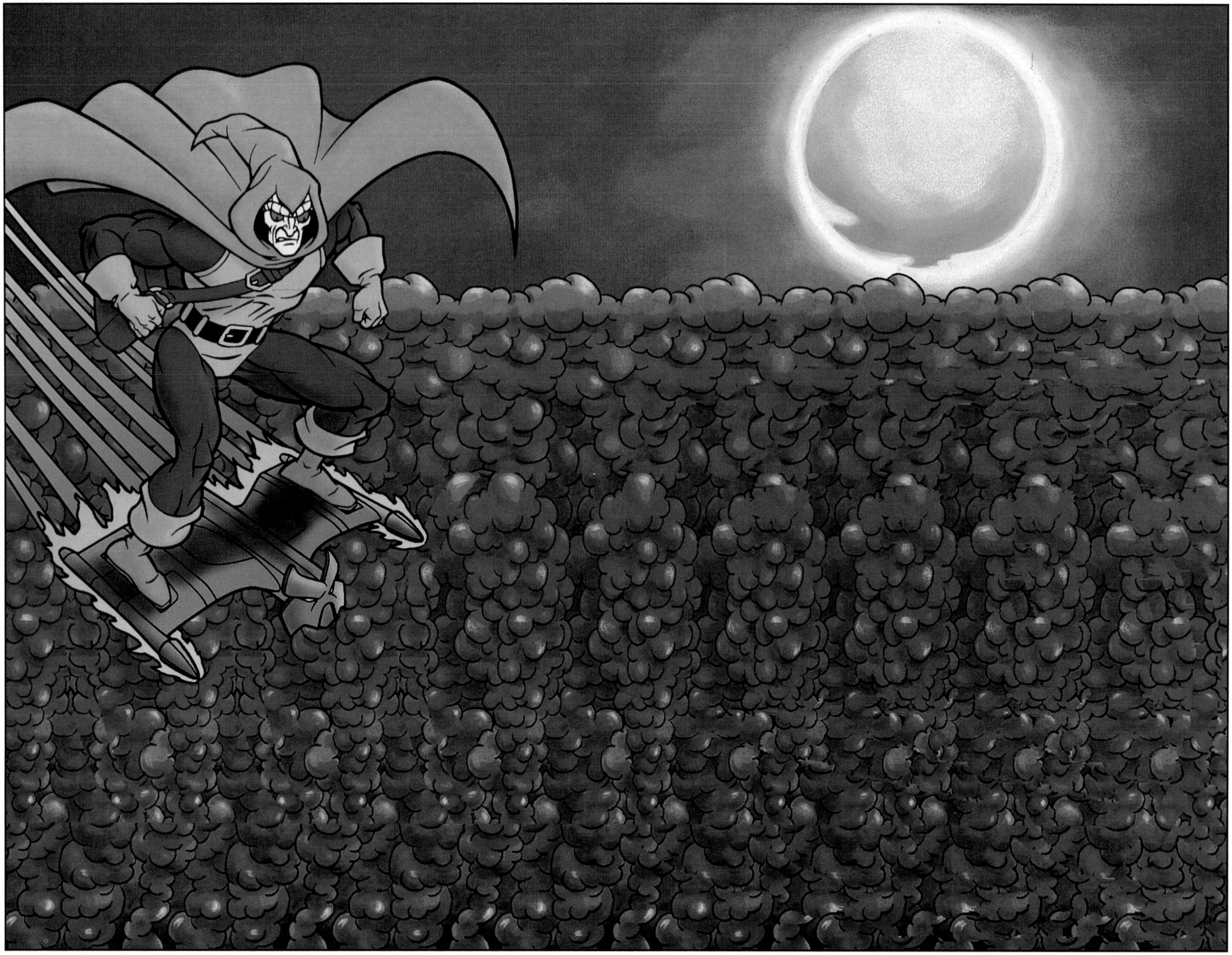

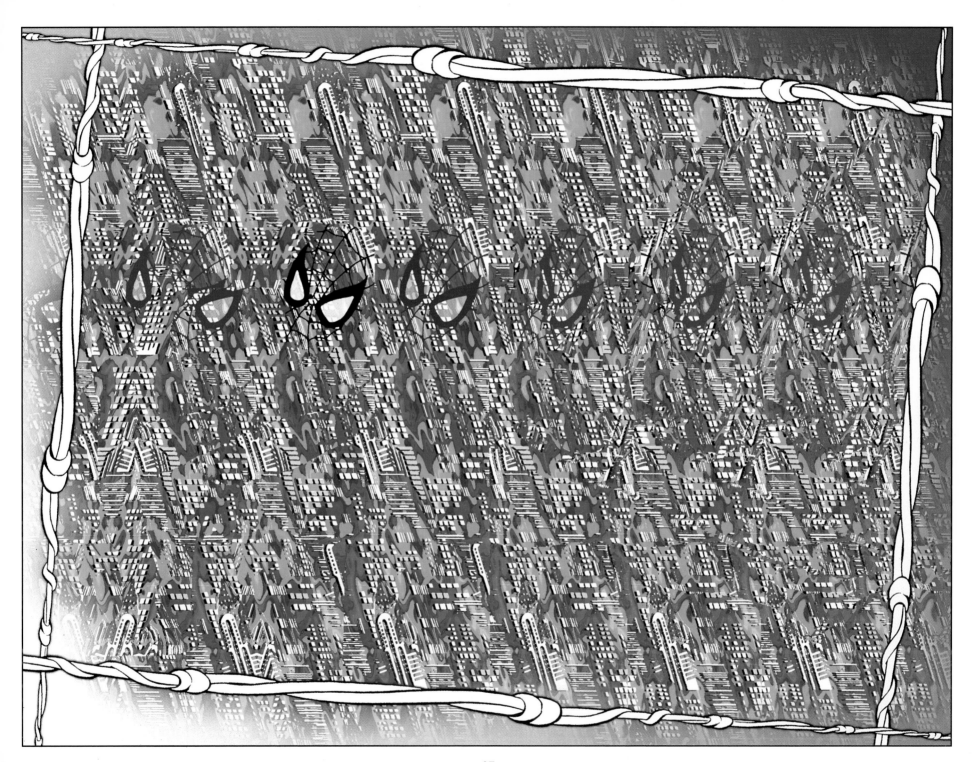

27

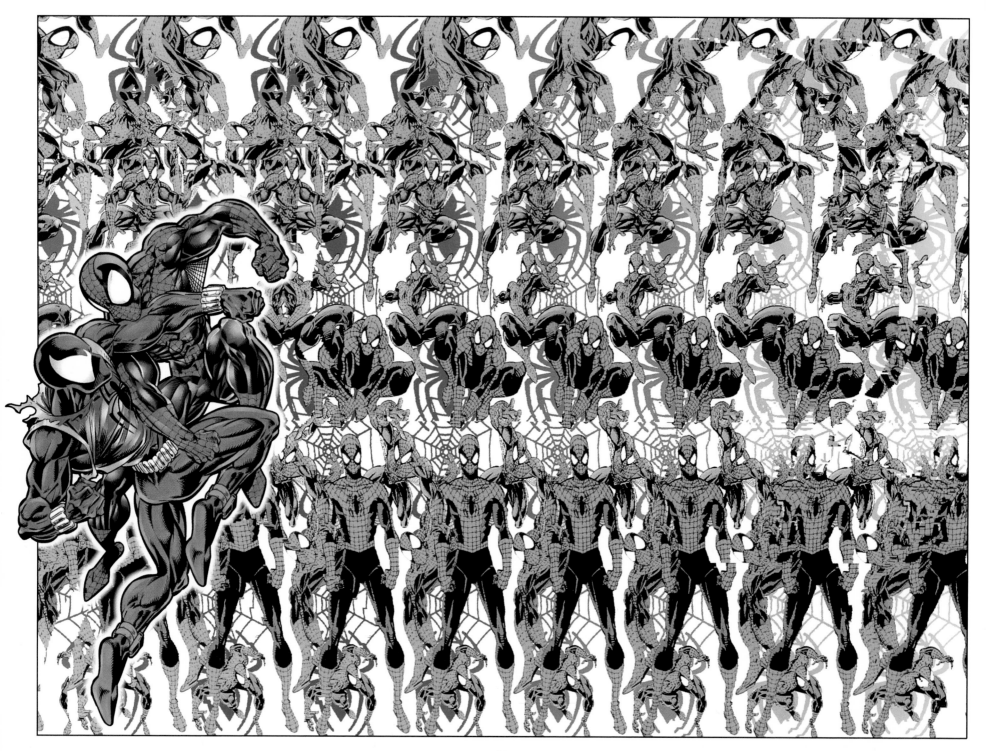

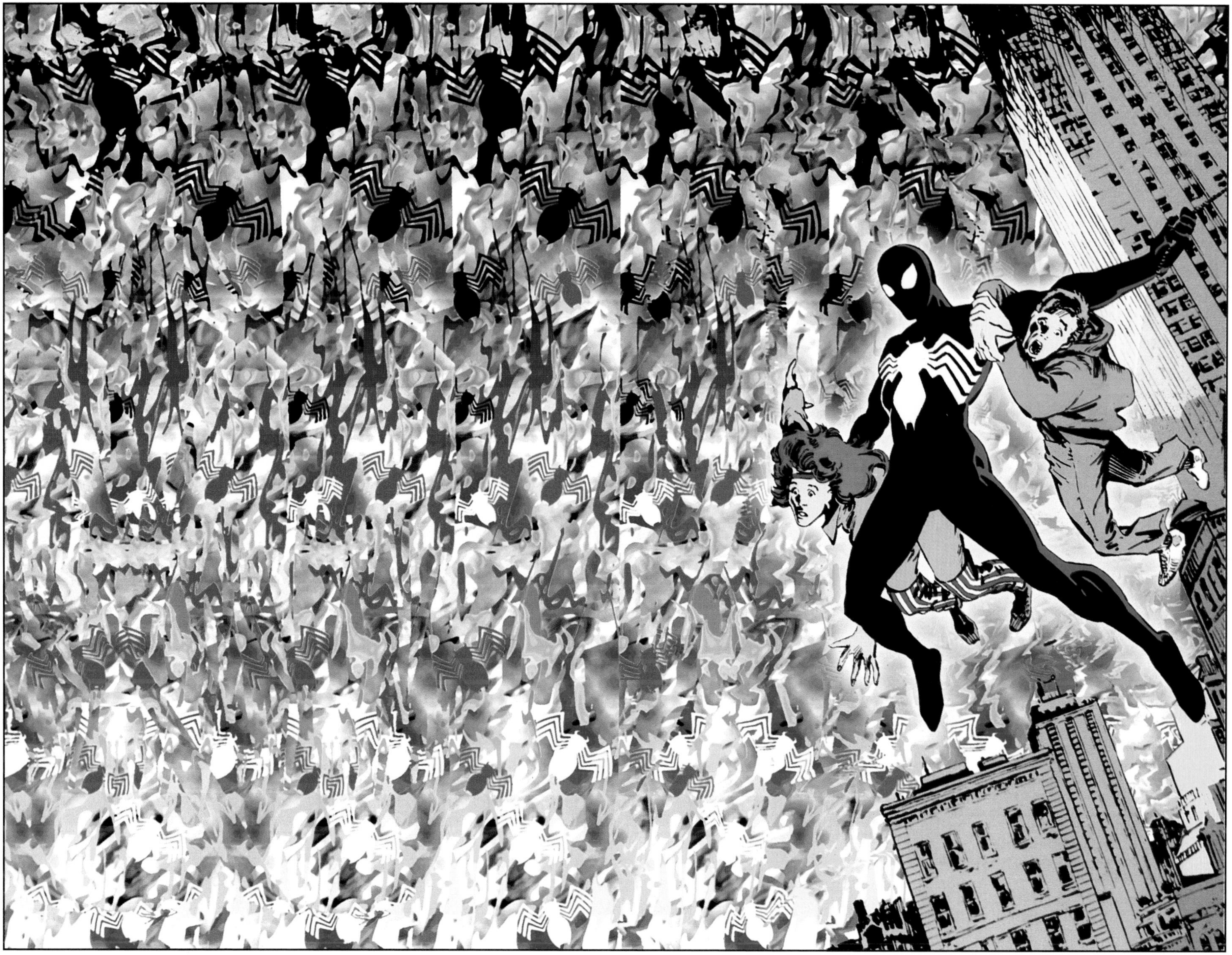

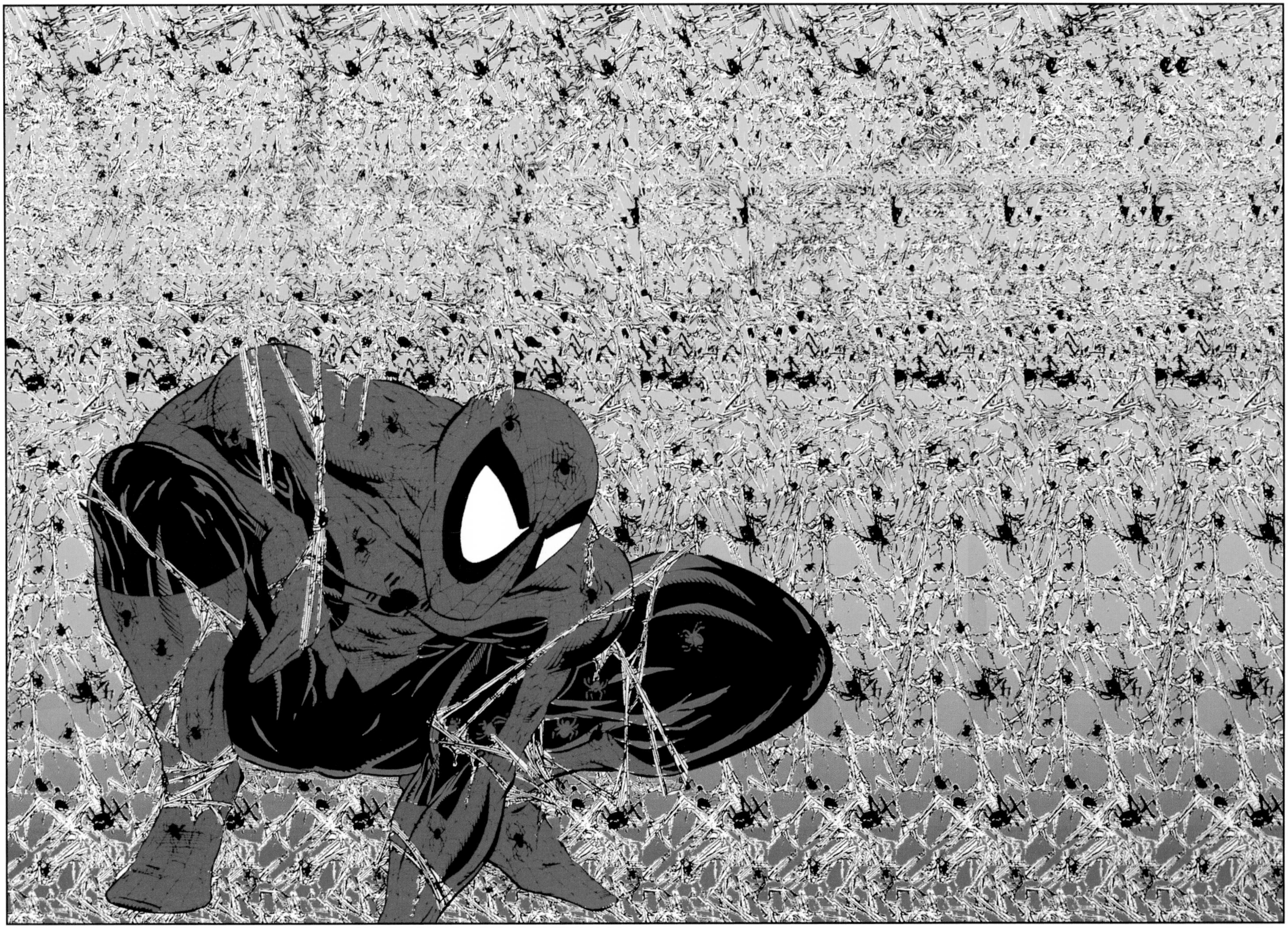

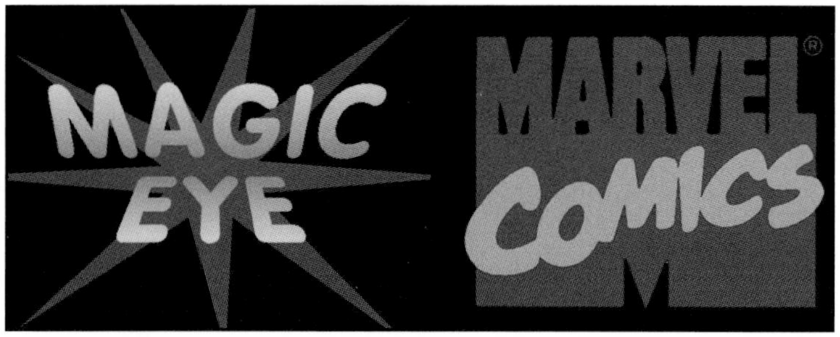
MAGIC
EYE
MARVEL
COMICS

Front Watermark

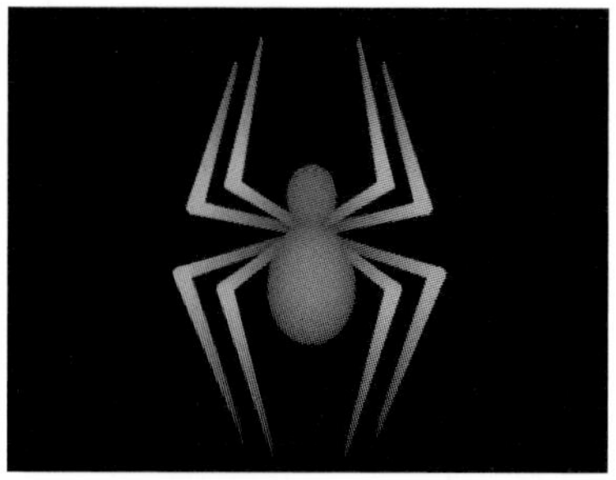

p. 5 Spider Symbol

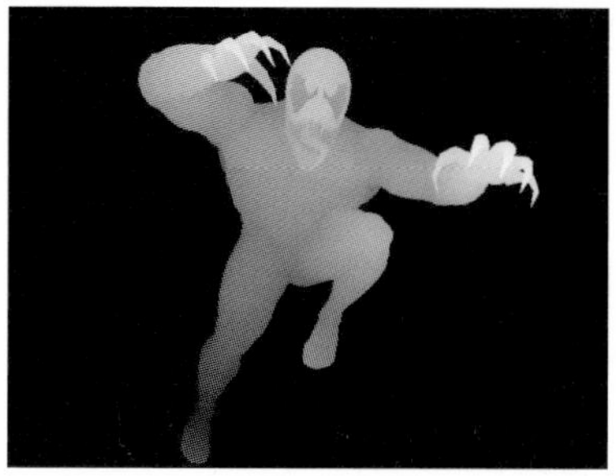

p. 6 Venom

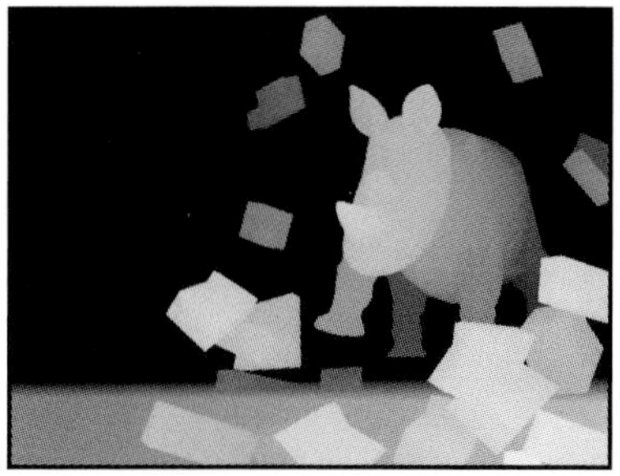

p. 7 Rhinoceros

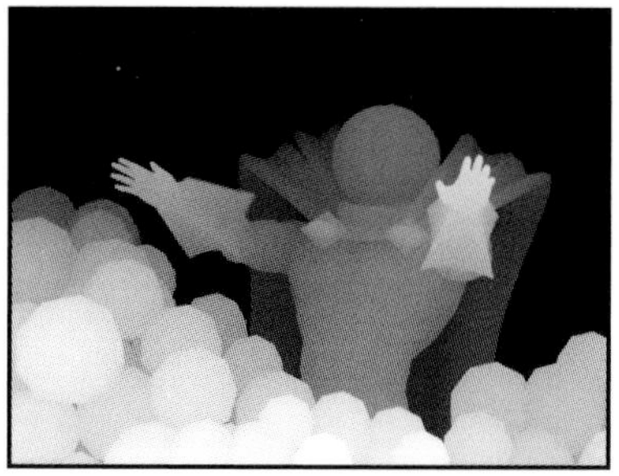

p. 8 Mysterio

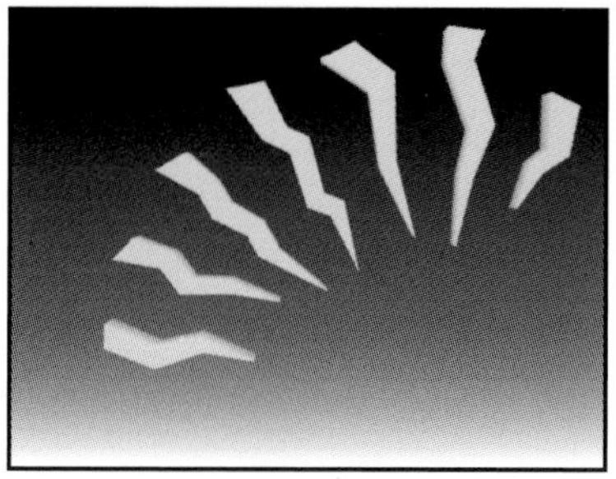

p. 9 Spider Sense

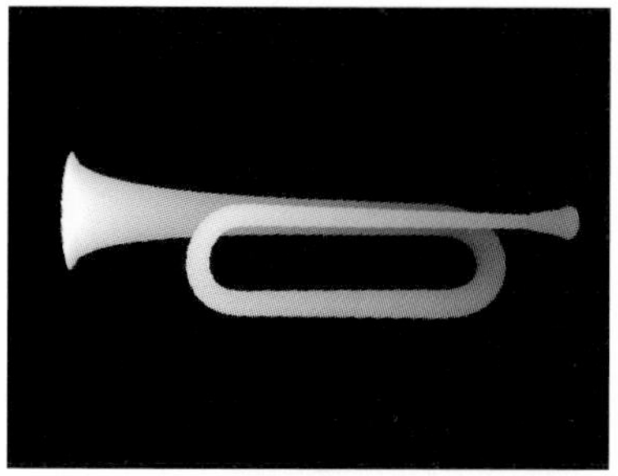

p. 10 Bugle

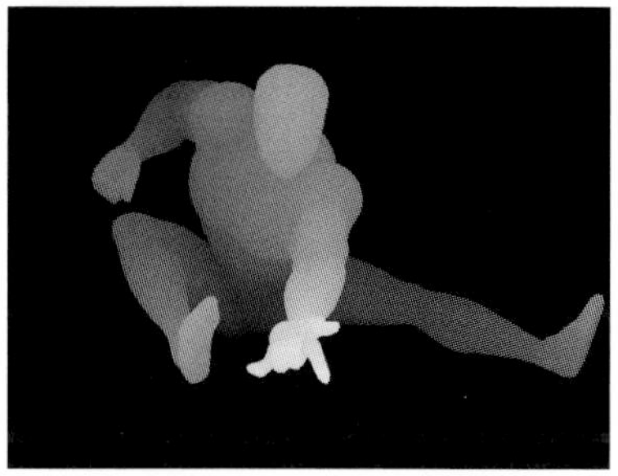

p. 11 Spiderman (avenger)

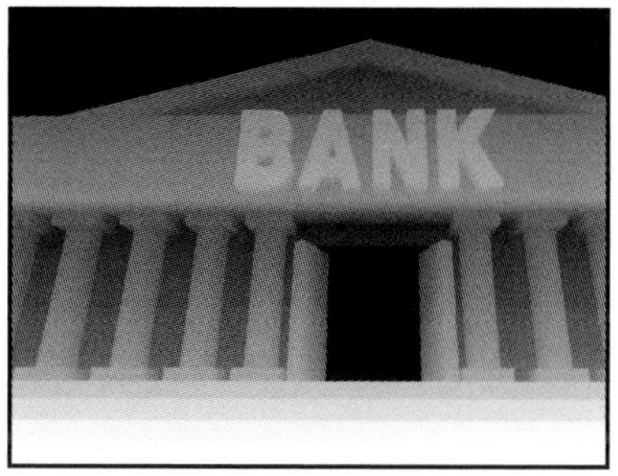
BANK

p. 12 Bank Doorway

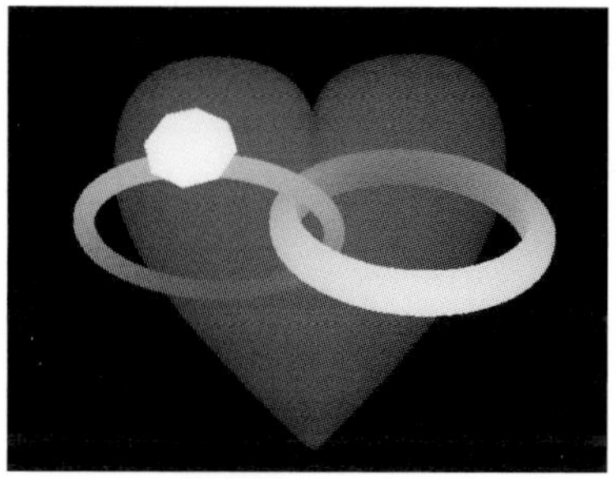

p. 13 Rings

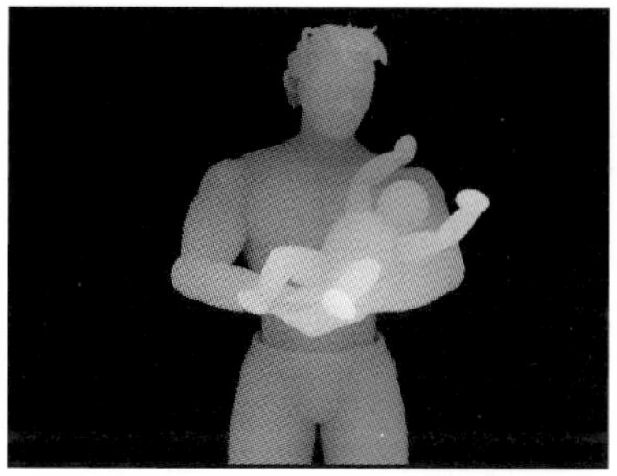

p. 14 Peter Holding Baby

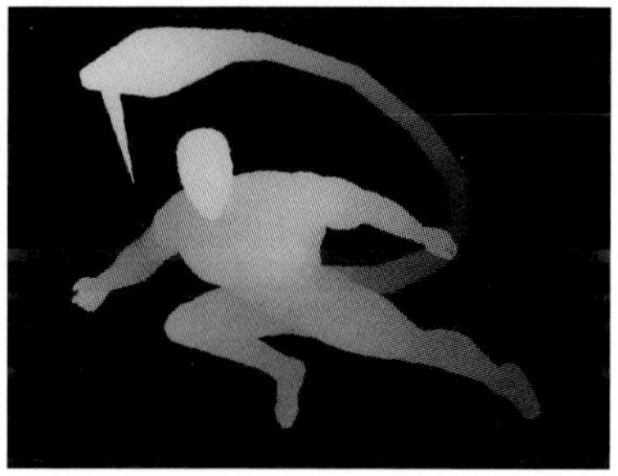

p. 15 Scorpion

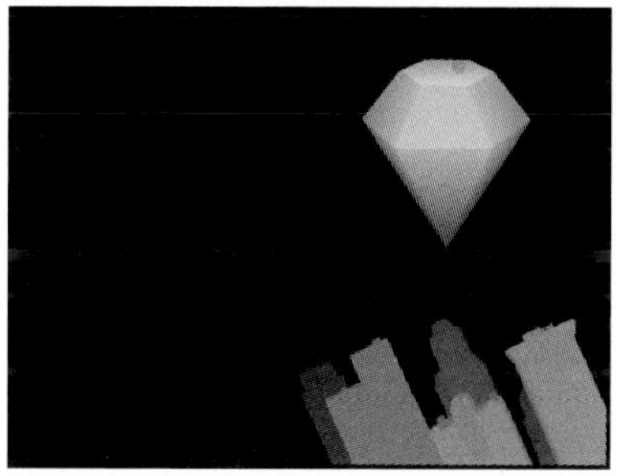

p. 16 Jewel
p. 17 Floater (no image)

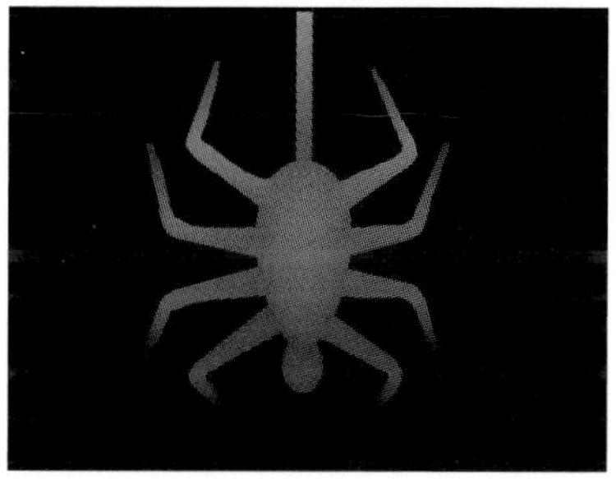

p. 18 Spider Symbol

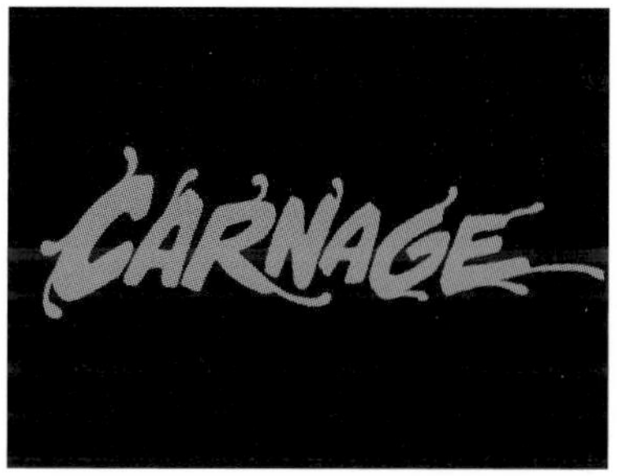
CARNAGE

p. 19 Carnage Logo

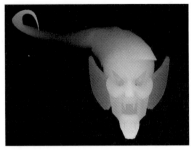

p. 20 Green Goblin

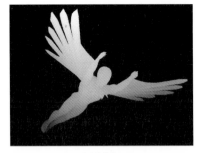

p. 21 Vulture

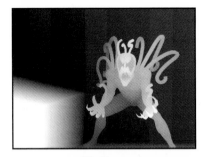

p. 22 Carnage

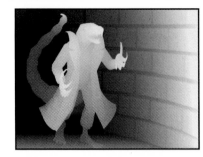

p. 23 Lizard

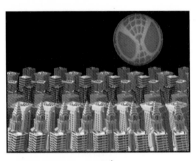

p. 24

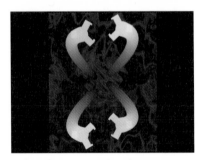

p. 25 Tentacles

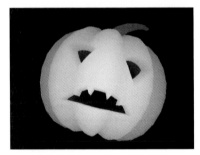

p. 26 Pumpkin Bomb

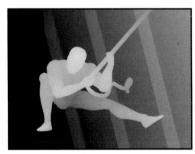

p. 27 Spiderman (swinging)

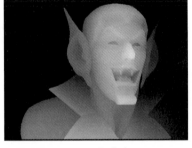

p. 28 Jackal

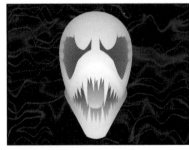

p. 29 Venom (head only)

SPIDER-MAN

p. 30 Spiderman Logo

MAGIC
EYE
MARVEL
COMICS

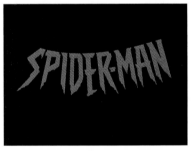

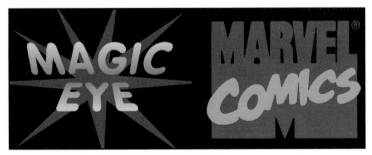

Back Watermark